Property Inventory Clerk

Training

And

Business Guide

By

Wise Tutor

PREFACE

Complete training book on how to become a professional inventory clerk and Start Inventory Business

Every strategy, tools, tips, and the technique you need to become a professional property inventory clerk!

If you're considering starting a property inventory business or you want to become a professional property inventory clerk this book is a must-read.

This book will teach and guide you with in-depth advice on building your inventory business and becoming a professional inventory clerk. The book imparts the practical and exciting strategies that professional property inventory clerks across the world are using to build significant cash flow through property inventory business.

The author 'Wise Tutor' has one goal in mind: to give you everything you need to become a professional property inventory clerk and be able to create a successful inventory business.

Wise Tutor

Property Inventory Clerk Training And Business Guide

Property Inventory Clerk Training And Business Guide

CONTENTS

Part 1

What is property inventory? 5

What is Check In?
Inventory & Check-in
Check out
Mid- Term inspection
The purpose of the inventory

Part 2

Why it is good to start an inventory business 13

Advantages of becoming an inventory clerk
What is an inventory report?

Part 3

What does an Inventory Clerk do? 19

Understanding 'fair wear and tear'
What is Schedule of condition?
Completing an inspection and completing a report.

Property Inventory Clerk Training And Business Guide

Photographs should be included in your report.

Inventory & Meter Readings

Part 4

Starting your own inventory business 25
Essential information to make ready for your client

Recognized governing bodies

Advantages of becoming member of a professional association

Be aware of the following

Reports Expectation

How to read a variety of meters

How to do the inventory check for a rental property

Property Inventory Clerk Training And Business Guide

Part 1

What is property inventory?

Inventory is a full detailed description of the contents in a property, from decorations, appliances, furniture, fixtures and fittings in the property including a full description of their condition and the condition of walls, ceilings, floors and carpets, light fittings, paintwork, windows, radiators etc.

Without an inventory being done for a property the landlord may have no recourse against the tenant or their deposits should there be any damages when they vacate the property, or else you may have to bear the costs for damages incurred by the tenants during their stay alone and repairing a whole lot of damage done in the property out of the landlord's own pocket.

If an experienced clerk visits a property and carry out a full inventory of its contents and prepare schedule of condition for all rooms, including outbuildings, garden and garages, he or she will compiled reports precisely and clearly detailing the contents

Property Inventory Clerk Training And Business Guide

found in the property and their condition with supporting pictures. This will be explained further in this book.

What is Check In?

Check In - This is when an Inventory Clerk who would have a copy of your report and keys to the property meet with the tenants at the property and go through the inventory report with them room by room, highlighting any issues and make note of any additional comments to the inventory where necessary. The clerk will take utility meter readings, and then hand over the keys to the tenant and getting them to sign the report agreeing on the condition of the property.

Inventory & Check-in

This is a combined Inventory and Check-In service when a clerk visits the property to carry out an inventory on the same day, just before tenants arrive or move in, and also go through what has been inspected with the tenants and handed over the property keys to them. Inventory companies usually offer this on a reduced rate thereby saving the client some money, instead of making two separate visits booking, only one visit by the clerk is required.

Check out

This is carried out at the end of a tenancy; the clerk compares the state of the property with the initial inventory done at check in, detailing any changes which may have arisen with a comparison with the initial check-in report, listing all changes, and make recommendations based on their professional expertise; the clerk will also note the state of cleanliness and if necessary further cleaning maybe required. Final meter readings are then taken.

The Check-Out Inspection takes place on the final day of the Tenancy term or on a date and time as close as possible to the last day of the Tenancy(where practicable) it could be after they already moved out of the property or before.

Usually at the time of the Check-Out Inspection the Tenant should have completed removing all personal items and all cleaning should be completed. And at the conclusion of the Check-Out Inspection the Tenant should return all keys belonging to the property and leave the flat for the last time. The Inventory Clerk will return the keys to the relevant Agent or any other third party as instructed.

During Check-Out Inspection the original Inventory & Schedule of Conditions will be checked in full. Any differences and missing items are recorded and the main issues highlighted to the Tenant. Photographs of any damages and general photographs will also be taken at this time.

It is not a necessity that the Landlord/Tenant attends the Check-Out Inspection, although if a Tenant is in attendance it does allow them to provide answers to any queries for example, if items cannot be found or damages are noted.

At the end of the Check-Out Inspection the meters are read, the keys counted and checked and the Tenants forwarding address recorded. A schedule is also completed highlighting the main points. Most clerks now use audio recording devise during all inspections to record notes which they will later transcribe. This also saves them time writing on the spot.

The Check-Out Report is then typed up and returned to the Landlord/Agent/Tenant normally within 48/72 hours, some were able to return within 24hours. At this point the Tenant/Landlord/Agent will discuss the Report with a view to reaching an agreement on the return of the Tenants deposit with any possible deductions highlighted

Mid- Term inspection

This is a valuable option for landlords and estate agents who wish to check the condition of their property where the tenant has been in place for at least three months or for a prolonged period of time, to find out how they are treating the property and whether any suggestions need to be made to them, or if there are any maintenance issues that may need your attention..

The purpose of the inventory

An inventory is there to protect both the tenant and the landlord. A property owner (Landlord) wishes to protect themselves from the costs of potential misuse of, or accidental damage of their properties by tenants. Tenants also wish to protect improper deductions from their deposits at the end of a tenancy. Therefore an agreed inventory carried out by an independent inventory clerk should ensure proof and evidence of the condition of a property at the start of a tenancy. At the end of a tenancy landlords and tenants are able to rely on the report as an agreed and definitive basis of comparison of the property at the end of a tenancy.

In United Kingdom, landlord no longer controls the tenant's deposit. Landlords securing a tenancy after April 2007 are subject to the Tenancy Deposit Scheme (TDS).

Under this initiative, they must place their tenant's deposit into either a Custodial or Insurance scheme run by an independent provider. Discrepancies arise when there is a dispute regarding the return of the deposit, often to do with issues surrounding property damage.

'Sufficient damage' refers to damage that is caused unfairly, and is opposed to Fair Wear and Tear. This is, as the House of Lords described it, "reasonable use of the premises by the tenant and the ordinary operation of natural forces".

Property Inventory Clerk Training And Business Guide

This is a contentious area because wear and tear can be a subjective matter. However, a detailed property inventory, perhaps composed by an experienced inventory clerk, should ensure appropriate standards of wear and tear are defined.

Therefore, tenants are now reliant on the inventory to get their deposit back. Therefore tenants no longer have to worry about losing your deposit because few landlords have dubious financial intentions. Also is the having not to worry.

Both the landlord and tenant including the letting agent should have copies of the inventory with schedule of the condition report.

The property inventory is part of the tenancy agreement between the landlord and the tenant, and as such, it is expected that all defects must be carefully noted in the inventory to ensure that the landlord can prove a tenant caused harm to the property, which subsequently led to refurbishment, repair and/or cleaning costs.

Property Inventory Clerk Training And Business Guide

A detailed property inventory report must then be produced to prove exactly what damage was caused by the tenant, based on the condition of the premises prior to their arrival.

A detailed account of a property will include the condition of fixtures, fittings and decorations, including walls, carpets and equipment. It is not enough to list an array of items the property is equipped with, nor is it sufficient to simply say where a scratch or crack lies, but should also feature a full list of furniture and accessories, as well as an overview of the garden and outdoor vicinities.

Property Inventory Clerk Training And Business Guide

Part 2

Why it is good to start an inventory business

Demand for inventory clerk services is consistent and growing due to ever growing demand for rental properties. The role of a property inventory clerk has become more important for landlords and letting agents renting properties to tenants since the introduction of the UK government's Tenancy Deposit Scheme in 2007

It is frustrating for any landlord to be left covering the cost of damages or loss made to their property during their tenants' residency. Floors can be scuffed, carpets stained and doors unnecessarily snapped from their hinges, as well as basic furnishings disappearing, among many other inventory issues. But when it comes to returning a tenant's deposit, it is not as simple as taking the required fee from the sum. The landlord must be able to prove to both a court and a tenant that damage or loss has occurred.

Property Inventory Clerk Training And Business Guide

Inventory is what also covers the tenant from being penalized for damages that were already in place before they took up their residency, and thus, ensures landlords do not miss sufficient damage caused by a former tenant.

It is then most advisable for landlords to invest in a property inventory that could save them a lot of unnecessary, and often unfair, expenses.

The greatest reason for this is the fact that it gives landlords a level of security when claiming a fee from a tenant's deposit. It also ensures tenants are not held responsible for loss or damage they did not cause, which helps promote a healthy relationship between them and the landlord.

A detailed inventory will help speed up negotiations regarding deposits, and makes the process easier. Lastly, a property inventory will ensure tenants realize the landlord values their property and takes offences against it seriously. This should go towards encouraging them to take good care of their accommodation.

Therefore a correctly compiled inventory is essential for all rental properties to enable a fair assessment of condition and level of cleanliness at the start and end of any tenancy term.

Advantages of becoming an inventory clerk

One of the many advantages of doing inventory business is that you don't need any previous experience or formal qualifications to become an inventory clerk (At the time of writing this book there are no formal qualifications)

All you need is some basic knowledge of the work which you will get from this book in order to produce accurate and professional reports to clients.

When working as an Inventory Clerk you are paid a fee for each inspection/report. The average fee is about £100 and it doesn't matter how quickly you can do the job. Once you gain some experience you'll be able to do an inspection of more property within the day and go back home to prepare the reports for faster delivery to your clients.

- You are your own boss.

- You can build a business with a substantial client base and sell it for a lot of money.

- You are free to refuse business from a client who gives you grief.

- You can decide to be flexible and work as a freelance Inventory Clerk
  - You get to decide when to work.
  - You decide how many hours to work

- You decide how much you get paid as it's you who sets the fees.

- You are an important party within the property letting business.

- There's always a demand for your work.

What is an inventory report?

An inventory report is the document that records the state of the property and its contents before you move in. it is a detailed inspection of the fixtures, fittings and furnishings in a property, including descriptive and conditional comments for each room. The report includes schedule of condition and an overview picture of each room and conditional photos for items that appear damaged or valuable.

As already stated in this book, It's the main document used to resolve any issues at the end of tenancy and can strongly influence what deductions (if any) are made from tenant's deposit.

Property Inventory Clerk Training And Business Guide

Property Inventory Clerk Training And Business Guide

Part 3

What does an Inventory Clerk do?

The main role of an inventory clerk is to inspect a property, collect evidence (take pictures) (photographs or video) and prepare an unbiased report of the contents and condition of the property prior to a property being let to tenants. At the end of a tenancy a further role is to re-inspect the property, collect evidence and prepare a further report to record any changes that have occurred at the property throughout the tenancy period. These changes may include damages, dilapidations and missing items etc.

Examples of what you will be doing:

You may be asked to pick up keys for the property to be inspected at the letting agent's office first, and to drop off the keys back at the Agent's office when you finish the inspection at the property.

Property Inventory Clerk Training And Business Guide

The types of properties you will be inspecting would range from studio apartments to large houses that may be furnished or unfurnished, part furnished or fully furnished flats, apartments and houses. You will need to be prepared for properties that are extensively furnished and include full sets of kitchen and dining ware. (Crockery, cutlery, cookware etc)

Understanding 'fair wear and tear'

As part of rental property check out list, parties involved should understand what's considered fair wear and tear, so they both know where they stand.

'Fair wear and tear' is the term used in lease agreements; it refers to the damage that happens through ordinary day-to-day use of the property, for example: the carpet being worn from people walking on it.

The UK House of Lords defines wear and tear as "Reasonable use of the premises by the tenant and the ordinary operation of natural forces"

So what forms of damage can be considered "reasonable" and naturally occurring, or unreasonable and beyond that of normal use?

Unfortunately, whether decorations, fixtures or fittings all deteriorate over time, therefore the condition of furniture, decorations and appliances can vary drastically depending on the age… that is the length of time] For that reason, the amount a landlord is entitled to when damage takes place will vary, too.

If tenant has not maintained a property to an acceptable standard, or have caused excessive damage due to neglect, or miss-use of the property, they will be liable for any repairs.

What is Schedule of condition?

The schedule of condition is part of the inventory report that states the condition of all the items listed on the inventory. This is where the shades of grey arise. It's a statement of fact to state that there's a sofa in the lounge, opinions on condition can differ. As stated earlier in this book, the inventory lists everything included in the rental property, such as the fixtures, fittings and furnishings (if the property is furnished).

Before a tenant move in, to check that everything listed on the inventory is present and correct. The clerk should also double check the condition of everything, and summarize all on the schedule of condition page.

Completing an inspection and completing a report.

Property Inventory clerks have different styles of working but there is always a journey between completing an inspection and completing a report. Some of the clerks' type their reports on the sport but this will slow you down if you are really going to be fast and timely in meeting other appointments for the same day, therefore many now take audio recordings and later transcribed it.

Property Inventory Clerk Training And Business Guide

Remember that an inventory clerk or inventory company might produce reports in several formats to suite different client needs.

Remember, how you can easily get familiar and increase your dictation confidence is by doing the inventory of your own house (where you live) inspect it thorough and prepare the report. You will see what your completed report looks like. You could the observed where and why it looks less professional and re-adjusts in that area in your next trial inspection. Practice, practice and practice the steps until you are satisfy with the type of report you have generated.

Photographs should be included in your report.

A professional inventory or check out reports should include pictures. A selection of photographs should be taken of every property, to include meters and keys etc. and to highlight any specific areas that may benefit from illustration further to the written Inventory document.

Property Inventory Clerk Training And Business Guide

Inventory & Meter Readings

As with standard Inventory report, Inventory and Meter Readings report can be produced at any time during the tenancy but is also enhanced with readings for the gas, electricity and occasionally water meters, supported with photos.

The Inventory Clerk should be in possession of a number of keys like "FB Keys/TBar keys/gas meter keys" etc in order to make your job easier and professional. Having the key which allow access to most meter cupboards is recommended, and these keys can be easily purchases at most tools stores.

In the event the meters cannot be found on the day of the Inspection this will be recorded on the report and the Tenant/Landlord will contact the relevant utility company to arrange for readings to be taken.

Property Inventory Clerk Training And Business Guide

Part 4

Starting your own inventory business:

Essential information to make ready for your client

As an Inventory provider you should make readily available the clear terms and conditions of providing your service, this should include:

1. You will have to create a sample report. A sample report that will serve as a marketing tool. Many new clients especially letting agents would ask to see a sample report before they can trust you to carry out a property check for them.

2. Have your situated business address on the report for credibility.

3. You must have a clear and transparent pricing structure – Your price list should be posted on your page. For example – post your standard price lists, and also post if there would be any additional charges if a standard property or bedroom you are to inspect have an extra en-suite, garage, shed, utility room,

extension, etc. these could incur additional charges as it will require the clerk to spend more time producing your report. Although some clerk may waive the additional charges to attract client.

4. Remember that when providing actual reports for review they will contain private information and are therefore confidential documents subject to the Data Protection Act. Make sure this was addressed in your terms and conditions.

5. Register with a governing body

Recognized governing bodies

Ii is good that inventory provider should be a member of a professional association. There are independent and none independent governing bodies, some are well recognized and some promotes their own inventory clerks.

Advantages of becoming member of a professional association:

Property Inventory Clerk Training And Business Guide

Most associations have an assessment process that applicants sample report must pass before they are granted membership. This means that, once you have demonstrated that you have the requisite experience, knowledge and skills, you may join the association and add the appropriate letters to your CV, business card or website. Membership shows that you have reached a certain level of expertise in your profession, and adds to your credibility. It also shows that you are serious about your business and professional development. But remember just being a card carrying member of an organization doesn't mean that this will automatically produce results for you – and you need to analyze the different types of professional bodies or institutes and chose carefully.

Information and Advice

Many institutions have web sites offering members password protected access to the industry news, surveys, reports, updates, career information, jobs, and details of events.

Networking Opportunities

An association may have regional networking and professional development events that you can attend, which can be useful for making new contacts and learning more about what's happening in the sector. National expos and conferences also offer excellent networking and research opportunities. If you wish to raise your profile you can volunteer to join committees and help organize events.

Be aware of the following:

A competent clerk should have been trained and certified by one of the governing bodies

Another good thing about this business is if you have been a tenant, landlord, estate or letting agent before or at present, then you could understand the relevant details expected when or what might become an issue for a tenant, landlord or agent on the report they want you to compile. Therefore produce a clear and clean report in such a way as to minimize the chances of disputes.

Reports Expectation

The property report should appear clear, structured with numbered items which is a reflection of high industry standards, with but not overwhelming photographs of the overview of the room.

It is an industry standard to number the items in the report and ideally separate descriptions from conditions in order to create easy comparison at Check Out.

Property Inventory Clerk Training And Business Guide

The report should have sufficient detail descriptions with conditions and individual items numbered.

How to read a variety of meters

(A)

Reading digital electricity meter

Example of meter screen;

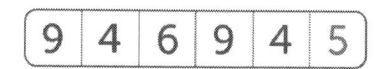

| 9 | 4 | 6 | 9 | 4 | 5 |

Example: This meter reading would be 94694

| 9 | 4 | 6 | 9 | 4 | 5̸ |

A digital electricity meter shows the current meter reading on a digital display. Here's how to read it:

1. Read the meter display from left to right.

2. Ignore any numbers in red and anything that appears after a decimal point or space.

Economy 7/Domestic Economy meters

If it is an Economy 7 or Domestic Economy meter, you'll have two rows of figures on the digital display:

'**Low**' is the reading for night or off-peak units.

'**Normal**' is the reading for day or peak-time units.

You read your meter the same as a standard digital electricity meter.

Property Inventory Clerk Training And Business Guide

(B)

Reading Dial electricity meter

Example of meter screen;

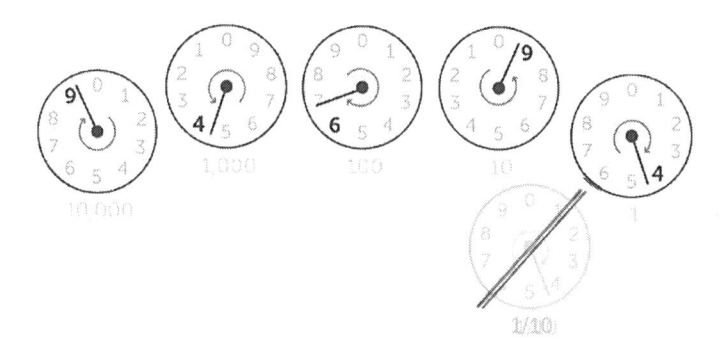

Some older electricity meters have dials instead of a row of numbers. They're simple to read, but it may help you to write down the numbers as you go.

Read the dials from left to right. Ignore the dial marked 1/10 or in red.

1. If the pointer on a dial is between two numbers, write down the lower number. But if the pointer is **between zero and nine**, it will **always be nine**. This is the case for the first and fourth dial on the diagram shown.

Property Inventory Clerk Training And Business Guide

2. If the pointer is exactly on a number but the reading on the dial after it is nine, take one away from that number. On the diagram shown the pointer on the third dial is exactly on the seven. But the reading on the fourth dial is a nine. So the reading on the third dial becomes six.

In the example shown, this meter reading would be 94694.

(C)

Reading Two-rate meters

Example of meter screen;

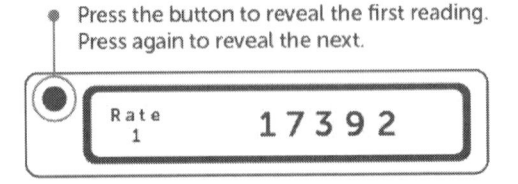

Press the button to reveal the first reading. Press again to reveal the next.

Rate 1   17392

Property Inventory Clerk Training And Business Guide

Some electricity properties still use meters that show two readings when you press a button on the meter. You may find a two-rate meter if the property has Economy 7, Economy 10 or Evening and Weekend tariff. But that is not your concern anyway.

Once you're at your meter display:

1. Press the button on the front of your meter.//
2. The meter will show each reading with a label next to it. This could be 'R1' and 'R2', '1' and '2', 'L' and 'N' or even 'low' and 'normal' which is the day reading and which is the night, depends on how the meter is set up.

Remember to always include each meter serial number with any meter that you're adding to the report. The serial numbers are usually found on the front of most meters. It may be on a sticker.

How to do the inventory check for a rental property

Take a tour of the property, prior to moving in, with the letting agent, inventory clerk or the landlord. Both of you should have copies of the inventory and the schedule of the condition.

Start from the front of the property including garden if applicable, then the front entrance, door, floor, wall, ceiling, and all fixtures and fittings in the property.

Note down the condition and take pictures or video to support when preparing the report. If is a check-out that is after the of a tenancy period, Note down the condition and take picture of any discrepancies between the inventory and reality, then notify any discrepancies back to the agent or landlord immediately in writing.

Have the landlord or the lettings agent draw up an up-to-date inventory to reflect the discrepancies, and only sign it once you're happy with it. If you sign beforehand, there's very little you can do if the landlord doesn't fix what needs fixing, or accuses you of causing the damage.

Property Inventory Clerk Training And Business Guide

The property inventory and the schedule of conditions then form part of the terms of your tenancy agreement.

If you wish to use photographs to support any discrepancy, or to highlight the condition of any existing damage, ensure you both sign and date each photograph.

Printed in Great Britain
by Amazon